50 Easy Weeknight Dinner Recipes for Home

By: Kelly Johnson

Table of Contents

- One-Pan Lemon Herb Chicken
- Beef and Broccoli Stir-Fry
- Creamy Tomato Basil Pasta
- Chicken Fajitas
- Teriyaki Salmon
- Sheet Pan BBQ Shrimp and Veggies
- Beef Tacos
- Spinach and Ricotta Stuffed Shells
- Chicken Alfredo
- Sweet and Sour Pork
- Vegetable Fried Rice
- Baked Ziti
- Chicken Stir-Fry with Snow Peas
- Sloppy Joes
- Lemon Garlic Shrimp Pasta
- Ground Turkey Chili
- BBQ Chicken Pizza
- Stuffed Bell Peppers
- One-Pot Chicken and Rice
- Veggie Quesadillas
- Pesto Pasta with Cherry Tomatoes
- Chicken and Vegetable Curry
- Beef Stroganoff
- Baked Chicken Parmesan
- Creamy Mushroom Risotto
- Greek Chicken Gyros
- Chicken Tortilla Soup
- Spaghetti Carbonara
- Tuna Casserole
- Beef and Bean Burritos
- Chicken Caesar Wraps
- Simple Meatball Sub Sandwiches
- Shrimp Scampi
- Chicken Pot Pie
- Sausage and Peppers Pasta

- Thai Peanut Chicken
- Pork Chops with Apples and Onions
- One-Pot Pasta Primavera
- Chicken and Black Bean Enchiladas
- Buffalo Chicken Salad
- Creamy Garlic Parmesan Orzo
- Fish Tacos with Lime Crema
- Stuffed Zucchini Boats
- Chicken Cacciatore
- Sweet Chili Meatballs
- Broccoli and Cheddar Stuffed Chicken
- Spicy Sausage Pasta
- Cheesy Chicken and Rice Bake
- Shrimp and Grits
- BBQ Meatloaf

One-Pan Lemon Herb Chicken

Ingredients:

- 4 bone-in, skin-on chicken thighs
- 2 tbsp olive oil
- Juice and zest of 1 lemon
- 2 tsp dried thyme
- 2 tsp dried rosemary
- 4 garlic cloves, minced
- Salt and pepper to taste
- 1 cup baby potatoes, halved
- 1 cup baby carrots

Instructions:

1. **Preheat Oven:** Preheat oven to 400°F (200°C).
2. **Prepare the Chicken:** In a bowl, mix olive oil, lemon juice, lemon zest, thyme, rosemary, garlic, salt, and pepper. Rub mixture over chicken thighs.
3. **Arrange Ingredients:** Place chicken thighs in a single layer on a baking sheet. Arrange baby potatoes and carrots around the chicken.
4. **Bake:** Bake for 35-40 minutes, or until chicken reaches an internal temperature of 165°F (74°C) and vegetables are tender.

Beef and Broccoli Stir-Fry

Ingredients:

- 1 lb flank steak, thinly sliced
- 2 tbsp vegetable oil
- 4 cups broccoli florets
- 1/2 cup beef broth
- 1/4 cup soy sauce
- 2 tbsp oyster sauce
- 2 tbsp cornstarch mixed with 2 tbsp water (slurry)
- 2 garlic cloves, minced
- 1 tsp fresh ginger, minced

Instructions:

1. **Cook the Beef:** Heat vegetable oil in a large skillet or wok over medium-high heat. Add beef and cook until browned, about 3-4 minutes. Remove from skillet and set aside.
2. **Stir-Fry Vegetables:** In the same skillet, add broccoli, garlic, and ginger. Stir-fry for 2-3 minutes until broccoli is tender-crisp.
3. **Add Sauce:** Return beef to the skillet. Add beef broth, soy sauce, and oyster sauce. Stir in cornstarch slurry and cook until sauce has thickened, about 1-2 minutes.
4. **Serve:** Serve over rice or noodles.

Creamy Tomato Basil Pasta

Ingredients:

- 12 oz pasta (penne or fettuccine)
- 2 tbsp olive oil
- 1 small onion, chopped
- 3 garlic cloves, minced
- 1 can (14.5 oz) diced tomatoes
- 1/2 cup heavy cream
- 1/2 cup grated Parmesan cheese
- 1/4 cup fresh basil, chopped
- Salt and pepper to taste

Instructions:

1. **Cook Pasta:** Cook pasta according to package instructions. Drain and set aside.
2. **Prepare Sauce:** In a large skillet, heat olive oil over medium heat. Sauté onion and garlic until softened, about 3-4 minutes.
3. **Add Tomatoes and Cream:** Stir in diced tomatoes and bring to a simmer. Reduce heat and stir in heavy cream and Parmesan cheese. Simmer for 2-3 minutes until sauce thickens.
4. **Combine:** Toss pasta with sauce and fresh basil. Season with salt and pepper. Serve hot.

Chicken Fajitas

Ingredients:

- 1 lb chicken breast, thinly sliced
- 2 tbsp olive oil
- 1 red bell pepper, sliced
- 1 yellow bell pepper, sliced
- 1 green bell pepper, sliced
- 1 onion, sliced
- 2 tbsp fajita seasoning
- 8 flour tortillas
- Optional toppings: sour cream, salsa, shredded cheese, lime wedges

Instructions:

1. **Cook the Chicken:** Heat olive oil in a large skillet over medium-high heat. Add chicken and fajita seasoning. Cook until chicken is no longer pink, about 5-7 minutes.
2. **Add Vegetables:** Add bell peppers and onion to the skillet. Cook, stirring occasionally, until vegetables are tender, about 5 minutes.
3. **Serve:** Warm tortillas and serve chicken and vegetables with optional toppings.

Teriyaki Salmon

Ingredients:

- 4 salmon fillets
- 1/2 cup teriyaki sauce
- 2 tbsp olive oil
- 2 garlic cloves, minced
- 1 tbsp fresh ginger, minced
- 1 tbsp sesame seeds
- 2 green onions, sliced

Instructions:

1. **Marinate the Salmon:** In a small bowl, mix teriyaki sauce, olive oil, garlic, and ginger. Marinate salmon fillets in the mixture for at least 30 minutes.
2. **Cook the Salmon:** Preheat oven to 375°F (190°C). Place salmon on a baking sheet and bake for 15-20 minutes, or until salmon is cooked through.
3. **Garnish and Serve:** Sprinkle with sesame seeds and green onions before serving.

Sheet Pan BBQ Shrimp and Veggies

Ingredients:

- 1 lb large shrimp, peeled and deveined
- 2 cups bell peppers, chopped
- 1 cup red onion, chopped
- 2 tbsp olive oil
- 1/2 cup BBQ sauce
- 1 tsp smoked paprika
- Salt and pepper to taste

Instructions:

1. **Preheat Oven:** Preheat oven to 400°F (200°C).
2. **Prepare Shrimp and Veggies:** Toss shrimp, bell peppers, and red onion with olive oil, BBQ sauce, smoked paprika, salt, and pepper.
3. **Bake:** Spread mixture on a sheet pan and bake for 15-20 minutes, until shrimp are cooked and vegetables are tender.
4. **Serve:** Serve hot with your choice of side.

Beef Tacos

Ingredients:

- 1 lb ground beef
- 1 packet taco seasoning
- 1/2 cup water
- 8 taco shells
- Toppings: shredded lettuce, diced tomatoes, shredded cheese, sour cream, salsa

Instructions:

1. **Cook the Beef:** In a skillet over medium heat, cook ground beef until browned. Drain excess fat.
2. **Add Seasoning:** Stir in taco seasoning and water. Simmer for 5 minutes, until sauce thickens.
3. **Assemble Tacos:** Spoon beef mixture into taco shells and top with your choice of toppings. Serve immediately.

Spinach and Ricotta Stuffed Shells

Ingredients:

- 20 jumbo pasta shells
- 2 cups ricotta cheese
- 1 cup cooked spinach, squeezed dry and chopped
- 1/2 cup grated Parmesan cheese
- 1 cup shredded mozzarella cheese
- 1 cup marinara sauce
- 1 egg
- 1 tbsp fresh basil, chopped

Instructions:

1. **Cook Shells:** Cook pasta shells according to package instructions. Drain and let cool.
2. **Prepare Filling:** In a bowl, mix ricotta cheese, spinach, Parmesan cheese, egg, and basil.
3. **Stuff the Shells:** Fill each shell with the ricotta mixture and place in a baking dish.
4. **Add Sauce and Cheese:** Pour marinara sauce over shells and sprinkle with mozzarella cheese.
5. **Bake:** Bake at 375°F (190°C) for 25-30 minutes, until cheese is melted and bubbly.

Chicken Alfredo

Ingredients:

- 1 lb chicken breast, sliced into strips
- 12 oz fettuccine pasta
- 2 tbsp olive oil
- 2 cups heavy cream
- 1 cup grated Parmesan cheese
- 3 garlic cloves, minced
- 1/2 cup fresh parsley, chopped
- Salt and pepper to taste

Instructions:

1. **Cook Pasta:** Cook fettuccine according to package instructions. Drain and set aside.
2. **Cook Chicken:** In a skillet, heat olive oil over medium-high heat. Cook chicken strips until no longer pink, about 5-7 minutes. Remove from skillet.
3. **Prepare Alfredo Sauce:** In the same skillet, cook garlic until fragrant. Add heavy cream and bring to a simmer. Stir in Parmesan cheese and cook until sauce thickens.
4. **Combine:** Add chicken and pasta to the sauce, tossing to coat. Garnish with parsley before serving.

Sweet and Sour Pork

Ingredients:

- 1 lb pork tenderloin, cut into bite-sized pieces
- 1/2 cup flour
- 1/4 cup cornstarch
- 1 egg
- Vegetable oil for frying
- 1 cup pineapple chunks
- 1 bell pepper, chopped
- 1 onion, chopped
- 1 cup sweet and sour sauce

Instructions:

1. **Bread the Pork:** In a bowl, combine flour and cornstarch. Dip pork pieces in egg, then coat with flour mixture.
2. **Fry the Pork:** Heat vegetable oil in a skillet and fry pork pieces until golden and crispy. Drain on paper towels.
3. **Stir-Fry Vegetables:** In the same skillet, stir-fry bell pepper and onion until tender.
4. **Combine:** Add pineapple chunks, pork, and sweet and sour sauce to the skillet. Cook until heated through. Serve over rice.

Vegetable Fried Rice

Ingredients:

- 2 cups cooked rice, preferably cold
- 2 tbsp vegetable oil
- 1 cup mixed vegetables (carrots, peas, corn)
- 2 garlic cloves, minced
- 2 eggs, beaten
- 2 tbsp soy sauce
- 2 green onions, sliced

Instructions:

1. **Cook Vegetables:** Heat vegetable oil in a large skillet or wok. Add mixed vegetables and garlic, and cook for 3-4 minutes until tender.
2. **Add Eggs:** Push vegetables to one side of the skillet and pour beaten eggs into the other side. Scramble and cook until set.
3. **Add Rice and Soy Sauce:** Add cooked rice and soy sauce to the skillet. Stir to combine and cook until heated through.
4. **Garnish:** Sprinkle with green onions before serving.

Baked Ziti

Ingredients:

- 12 oz ziti pasta
- 2 cups marinara sauce
- 1 lb ground beef
- 1/2 cup grated Parmesan cheese
- 2 cups shredded mozzarella cheese
- 1 egg
- 1 cup ricotta cheese
- 1 tbsp fresh basil, chopped

Instructions:

1. **Cook Pasta:** Cook ziti according to package instructions. Drain and set aside.
2. **Prepare Meat Sauce:** In a skillet, cook ground beef until browned. Drain excess fat. Add marinara sauce and simmer for 10 minutes.
3. **Mix Cheeses:** In a bowl, mix ricotta cheese, egg, and basil.
4. **Assemble:** In a baking dish, combine cooked ziti with meat sauce and cheese mixture. Top with mozzarella cheese.
5. **Bake:** Bake at 375°F (190°C) for 25-30 minutes, until cheese is melted and bubbly.

Chicken Stir-Fry with Snow Peas

Ingredients:

- 1 lb boneless, skinless chicken breast, thinly sliced
- 2 cups snow peas
- 2 bell peppers, sliced
- 1 onion, sliced
- 3 tbsp vegetable oil
- 1/4 cup soy sauce
- 2 tbsp hoisin sauce
- 2 tbsp cornstarch mixed with 2 tbsp water (slurry)
- 2 garlic cloves, minced
- 1 tsp fresh ginger, minced

Instructions:

1. **Cook the Chicken:** Heat vegetable oil in a large skillet or wok over medium-high heat. Add chicken and cook until browned, about 5 minutes. Remove from skillet and set aside.
2. **Stir-Fry Vegetables:** In the same skillet, add garlic and ginger and cook until fragrant. Add bell peppers, onion, and snow peas. Stir-fry for 3-4 minutes.
3. **Add Sauce:** Return chicken to the skillet. Stir in soy sauce and hoisin sauce, then add cornstarch slurry. Cook until sauce has thickened and everything is well combined, about 2 minutes.
4. **Serve:** Serve over rice or noodles.

Sloppy Joes

Ingredients:

- 1 lb ground beef
- 1 small onion, chopped
- 1/2 cup ketchup
- 1/4 cup brown sugar
- 2 tbsp Worcestershire sauce
- 1 tbsp Dijon mustard
- 1/4 cup water
- 4 hamburger buns
- Salt and pepper to taste

Instructions:

1. **Cook the Beef:** In a large skillet, cook ground beef and onion over medium heat until beef is browned and onion is soft. Drain excess fat.
2. **Add Sauce Ingredients:** Stir in ketchup, brown sugar, Worcestershire sauce, Dijon mustard, and water. Simmer for 10 minutes until thickened.
3. **Serve:** Spoon mixture onto hamburger buns and serve hot.

Lemon Garlic Shrimp Pasta

Ingredients:

- 12 oz linguine or spaghetti
- 1 lb large shrimp, peeled and deveined
- 2 tbsp olive oil
- 4 garlic cloves, minced
- Juice and zest of 1 lemon
- 1/4 cup chopped fresh parsley
- 1/2 cup grated Parmesan cheese
- Salt and pepper to taste

Instructions:

1. **Cook Pasta:** Cook pasta according to package instructions. Drain and set aside.
2. **Cook Shrimp:** In a large skillet, heat olive oil over medium heat. Add garlic and cook until fragrant. Add shrimp and cook until pink and opaque, about 3-4 minutes per side.
3. **Combine:** Add cooked pasta, lemon juice, and zest to the skillet. Toss to combine. Stir in parsley and Parmesan cheese. Season with salt and pepper.
4. **Serve:** Serve immediately.

Ground Turkey Chili

Ingredients:

- 1 lb ground turkey
- 1 onion, chopped
- 2 garlic cloves, minced
- 1 can (15 oz) diced tomatoes
- 1 can (15 oz) kidney beans, drained and rinsed
- 1 can (15 oz) black beans, drained and rinsed
- 1 cup chicken broth
- 2 tbsp chili powder
- 1 tsp cumin
- Salt and pepper to taste

Instructions:

1. **Cook the Turkey:** In a large pot, cook ground turkey and onion over medium heat until turkey is browned and onion is soft. Add garlic and cook for another minute.
2. **Add Remaining Ingredients:** Stir in diced tomatoes, kidney beans, black beans, chicken broth, chili powder, and cumin.
3. **Simmer:** Bring to a boil, then reduce heat and simmer for 30 minutes, stirring occasionally. Season with salt and pepper.
4. **Serve:** Serve hot with your choice of toppings.

BBQ Chicken Pizza

Ingredients:

- 1 pre-made pizza dough
- 1 cup cooked chicken, shredded
- 1/2 cup BBQ sauce
- 1/2 red onion, thinly sliced
- 1 cup shredded mozzarella cheese
- 1/4 cup sliced fresh cilantro

Instructions:

1. **Preheat Oven:** Preheat oven to 450°F (230°C).
2. **Prepare Pizza:** Roll out pizza dough on a floured surface. Transfer to a pizza stone or baking sheet.
3. **Add Toppings:** Spread BBQ sauce over dough. Top with shredded chicken, red onion, and mozzarella cheese.
4. **Bake:** Bake for 12-15 minutes, or until crust is golden and cheese is bubbly.
5. **Garnish and Serve:** Sprinkle with fresh cilantro before serving.

Stuffed Bell Peppers

Ingredients:

- 4 large bell peppers, tops cut off and seeds removed
- 1 lb ground beef or turkey
- 1 cup cooked rice
- 1 can (14.5 oz) diced tomatoes
- 1/2 cup grated Parmesan cheese
- 1 cup shredded mozzarella cheese
- 1 tsp Italian seasoning
- Salt and pepper to taste

Instructions:

1. **Preheat Oven:** Preheat oven to 375°F (190°C).
2. **Prepare Filling:** In a large skillet, cook ground beef or turkey until browned. Stir in cooked rice, diced tomatoes, Parmesan cheese, Italian seasoning, salt, and pepper.
3. **Stuff Peppers:** Fill each bell pepper with the meat mixture and place in a baking dish.
4. **Bake:** Top with shredded mozzarella cheese and bake for 30-35 minutes, until peppers are tender.
5. **Serve:** Serve hot.

One-Pot Chicken and Rice

Ingredients:

- 4 bone-in, skin-on chicken thighs
- 1 cup long-grain rice
- 2 cups chicken broth
- 1 cup frozen peas
- 1 cup carrots, diced
- 1 onion, chopped
- 2 garlic cloves, minced
- 1 tsp dried thyme
- 1 tbsp olive oil
- Salt and pepper to taste

Instructions:

1. **Brown the Chicken:** Heat olive oil in a large pot over medium heat. Season chicken thighs with salt and pepper, and brown on both sides. Remove from pot and set aside.
2. **Cook Vegetables:** In the same pot, add onion, garlic, carrots, and cook until softened. Stir in rice and cook for 2 minutes.
3. **Add Broth and Chicken:** Return chicken to the pot and pour in chicken broth. Add thyme. Bring to a boil, then reduce heat to low and cover. Simmer for 20-25 minutes, until rice is cooked and chicken is tender.
4. **Add Peas:** Stir in frozen peas and cook for another 5 minutes. Serve hot.

Veggie Quesadillas

Ingredients:

- 4 large flour tortillas
- 1 cup shredded cheese (cheddar, mozzarella, or a blend)
- 1 cup bell peppers, chopped
- 1 cup mushrooms, sliced
- 1/2 cup red onion, chopped
- 1 cup spinach
- 2 tbsp olive oil
- Salt and pepper to taste

Instructions:

1. **Prepare Filling:** In a skillet, heat olive oil over medium heat. Sauté bell peppers, mushrooms, and red onion until tender. Stir in spinach until wilted. Season with salt and pepper.
2. **Assemble Quesadillas:** Place half of the cheese on one half of each tortilla. Top with sautéed vegetables and the remaining cheese. Fold tortilla in half.
3. **Cook:** Wipe out the skillet and heat over medium heat. Cook quesadillas for 2-3 minutes per side, until golden and cheese is melted.
4. **Serve:** Cut into wedges and serve with salsa or sour cream.

Pesto Pasta with Cherry Tomatoes

Ingredients:

- 12 oz pasta (penne, fusilli, or your choice)
- 1 cup pesto sauce
- 1 cup cherry tomatoes, halved
- 1/4 cup grated Parmesan cheese
- 2 tbsp olive oil
- Salt and pepper to taste
- Fresh basil leaves for garnish

Instructions:

1. **Cook Pasta:** Cook pasta according to package instructions. Drain and set aside.
2. **Combine Ingredients:** In a large bowl, toss cooked pasta with pesto sauce and cherry tomatoes.
3. **Serve:** Drizzle with olive oil and sprinkle with Parmesan cheese. Garnish with fresh basil leaves. Serve immediately.

Chicken and Vegetable Curry

Ingredients:

- 1 lb chicken breast, cubed
- 2 cups mixed vegetables (carrots, bell peppers, peas)
- 1 onion, chopped
- 3 garlic cloves, minced
- 1 tbsp fresh ginger, minced
- 2 tbsp curry powder
- 1 can (14 oz) coconut milk
- 2 tbsp vegetable oil
- Salt and pepper to taste

Instructions:

1. **Cook Chicken:** Heat vegetable oil in a large skillet over medium heat. Add chicken and cook until browned and cooked through. Remove from skillet and set aside.
2. **Prepare Curry Sauce:** In the same skillet, cook onion, garlic, and ginger until softened. Stir in curry powder and cook for 1 minute.
3. **Combine Ingredients:** Add mixed vegetables and coconut milk to the skillet. Bring to a simmer and cook until vegetables are tender. Return chicken to the skillet and cook until heated through.
4. **Serve:** Season with salt and pepper. Serve over rice or with naan bread.

Beef Stroganoff

Ingredients:

- 1 lb beef sirloin, thinly sliced
- 1 cup mushrooms, sliced
- 1 onion, chopped
- 2 garlic cloves, minced
- 1 cup beef broth
- 1 cup sour cream
- 2 tbsp flour
- 2 tbsp butter
- 2 tbsp olive oil
- Salt and pepper to taste

Instructions:

1. **Cook Beef:** In a large skillet, heat olive oil and butter over medium-high heat. Add beef and cook until browned. Remove from skillet and set aside.
2. **Prepare Sauce:** In the same skillet, cook onion, garlic, and mushrooms until softened. Stir in flour and cook for 1 minute.
3. **Combine Ingredients:** Add beef broth and bring to a simmer. Stir in sour cream and return beef to the skillet. Cook until heated through and sauce has thickened.
4. **Serve:** Serve over egg noodles or rice.

Baked Chicken Parmesan

Ingredients:

- 4 boneless, skinless chicken breasts
- 1 cup breadcrumbs
- 1/2 cup grated Parmesan cheese
- 1 cup marinara sauce
- 1 cup shredded mozzarella cheese
- 1/2 cup all-purpose flour
- 2 eggs, beaten
- 2 tbsp olive oil
- Salt and pepper to taste

Instructions:

1. **Preheat Oven:** Preheat oven to 375°F (190°C).
2. **Prepare Chicken:** Dredge chicken breasts in flour, dip in beaten eggs, and coat with a mixture of breadcrumbs and Parmesan cheese.
3. **Bake:** Place chicken on a baking sheet and drizzle with olive oil. Bake for 20 minutes.
4. **Add Toppings:** Top each chicken breast with marinara sauce and shredded mozzarella cheese. Bake for an additional 10 minutes, or until cheese is melted and bubbly.
5. **Serve:** Serve with pasta or a side salad.

Creamy Mushroom Risotto

Ingredients:

- 1 cup Arborio rice
- 1 cup mushrooms, sliced
- 1 onion, chopped
- 3 garlic cloves, minced
- 1/2 cup white wine (optional)
- 4 cups chicken or vegetable broth
- 1 cup grated Parmesan cheese
- 2 tbsp butter
- 2 tbsp olive oil
- Salt and pepper to taste

Instructions:

1. **Cook Mushrooms:** Heat olive oil and butter in a large skillet. Add mushrooms and cook until browned. Remove and set aside.
2. **Prepare Risotto:** In the same skillet, cook onion and garlic until softened. Add Arborio rice and cook, stirring frequently, until rice is lightly toasted.
3. **Add Liquid:** If using wine, add it now and cook until absorbed. Gradually add broth, one cup at a time, stirring constantly, until rice is creamy and cooked through.
4. **Combine Ingredients:** Stir in cooked mushrooms and Parmesan cheese. Season with salt and pepper. Serve hot.

Greek Chicken Gyros

Ingredients:

- 1 lb chicken thighs, boneless and skinless
- 1/4 cup olive oil
- 2 tbsp lemon juice
- 2 garlic cloves, minced
- 1 tbsp dried oregano
- 1 tsp ground cumin
- 1 tsp paprika
- Salt and pepper to taste
- Pita bread and tzatziki sauce for serving

Instructions:

1. **Marinate Chicken:** In a bowl, mix olive oil, lemon juice, garlic, oregano, cumin, paprika, salt, and pepper. Marinate chicken thighs in the mixture for at least 1 hour.
2. **Cook Chicken:** Preheat grill or skillet over medium-high heat. Cook chicken for 5-7 minutes per side, until fully cooked. Slice into strips.
3. **Serve:** Serve chicken in pita bread with tzatziki sauce and your choice of toppings.

Chicken Tortilla Soup

Ingredients:

- 1 lb chicken breast, cooked and shredded
- 1 can (15 oz) black beans, drained and rinsed
- 1 can (15 oz) diced tomatoes
- 1 cup corn kernels
- 1 onion, chopped
- 3 garlic cloves, minced
- 1 tbsp chili powder
- 1 tsp cumin
- 4 cups chicken broth
- 1 tbsp olive oil
- Tortilla strips and lime wedges for serving

Instructions:

1. **Cook Vegetables:** In a large pot, heat olive oil over medium heat. Cook onion and garlic until softened.
2. **Add Ingredients:** Stir in chili powder and cumin, then add black beans, diced tomatoes, corn, and chicken broth. Bring to a boil.
3. **Simmer:** Reduce heat and simmer for 15 minutes. Add shredded chicken and cook until heated through.
4. **Serve:** Serve with tortilla strips and lime wedges.

Spaghetti Carbonara

Ingredients:

- 12 oz spaghetti
- 4 oz pancetta or bacon, diced
- 2 large eggs
- 1 cup grated Parmesan cheese
- 2 garlic cloves, minced
- Salt and pepper to taste
- Fresh parsley for garnish (optional)

Instructions:

1. **Cook Pasta:** Cook spaghetti according to package instructions. Reserve 1/2 cup of pasta water and drain the rest.
2. **Cook Pancetta:** In a skillet, cook pancetta or bacon until crispy. Remove from skillet and set aside.
3. **Prepare Sauce:** In a bowl, whisk together eggs and Parmesan cheese.
4. **Combine:** Add cooked pasta to the skillet with pancetta, then remove from heat. Quickly stir in egg mixture, adding reserved pasta water as needed to create a creamy sauce.
5. **Serve:** Garnish with fresh parsley if desired. Serve immediately.

Tuna Casserole

Ingredients:

- 1 can (12 oz) tuna, drained
- 2 cups cooked egg noodles
- 1 cup frozen peas
- 1 can (10.5 oz) cream of mushroom soup
- 1/2 cup milk
- 1 cup shredded cheddar cheese
- 1/2 cup breadcrumbs
- 2 tbsp olive oil
- Salt and pepper to taste

Instructions:

1. **Preheat Oven:** Preheat oven to 375°F (190°C).
2. **Combine Ingredients:** In a large bowl, mix together tuna, cooked noodles, peas, cream of mushroom soup, milk, and cheddar cheese. Season with salt and pepper.
3. **Transfer to Dish:** Pour mixture into a greased baking dish.
4. **Top and Bake:** In a small bowl, mix breadcrumbs with olive oil and sprinkle over the casserole. Bake for 25-30 minutes, or until the top is golden and the casserole is heated through.
5. **Serve:** Serve hot.

Beef and Bean Burritos

Ingredients:

- 1 lb ground beef
- 1 can (15 oz) black beans, drained and rinsed
- 1 cup salsa
- 1 cup shredded cheddar cheese
- 4 large flour tortillas
- 1 tbsp taco seasoning
- 1 tbsp olive oil
- Sour cream and chopped cilantro for serving

Instructions:

1. **Cook Beef:** In a skillet, heat olive oil over medium heat. Add ground beef and cook until browned. Stir in taco seasoning.
2. **Add Beans and Salsa:** Add black beans and salsa to the skillet. Cook until heated through.
3. **Assemble Burritos:** Spoon beef mixture onto tortillas and sprinkle with cheddar cheese. Roll up tortillas to form burritos.
4. **Serve:** Serve with sour cream and chopped cilantro.

Chicken Caesar Wraps

Ingredients:

- 2 cups cooked chicken breast, sliced
- 1 cup romaine lettuce, chopped
- 1/2 cup Caesar dressing
- 1/4 cup grated Parmesan cheese
- 4 large flour tortillas
- Salt and pepper to taste

Instructions:

1. **Prepare Filling:** In a bowl, toss together chicken, lettuce, Caesar dressing, and Parmesan cheese.
2. **Assemble Wraps:** Place a portion of the filling in the center of each tortilla.
3. **Wrap:** Fold the sides of the tortilla over the filling and roll up tightly.
4. **Serve:** Cut in half if desired and serve immediately.

Simple Meatball Sub Sandwiches

Ingredients:

- 1 lb meatballs (store-bought or homemade)
- 1 cup marinara sauce
- 4 sub rolls
- 1 cup shredded mozzarella cheese
- 1/4 cup grated Parmesan cheese
- Fresh basil for garnish (optional)

Instructions:

1. **Preheat Oven:** Preheat oven to 375°F (190°C).
2. **Heat Meatballs:** In a saucepan, heat meatballs and marinara sauce until hot.
3. **Assemble Subs:** Place meatballs in sub rolls and top with marinara sauce. Sprinkle with mozzarella and Parmesan cheese.
4. **Bake:** Place subs on a baking sheet and bake for 10-12 minutes, or until cheese is melted and bubbly.
5. **Serve:** Garnish with fresh basil if desired.

Shrimp Scampi

Ingredients:

- 1 lb large shrimp, peeled and deveined
- 8 oz linguine or spaghetti
- 4 garlic cloves, minced
- 1/4 cup white wine (optional)
- 1/4 cup lemon juice
- 1/4 cup chopped fresh parsley
- 4 tbsp butter
- 2 tbsp olive oil
- Salt and pepper to taste

Instructions:

1. **Cook Pasta:** Cook linguine according to package instructions. Drain and set aside.
2. **Cook Shrimp:** In a large skillet, heat olive oil and 2 tbsp butter over medium heat. Add garlic and cook until fragrant. Add shrimp and cook until pink, about 2-3 minutes per side. Remove shrimp and set aside.
3. **Prepare Sauce:** In the same skillet, add white wine (if using) and lemon juice. Cook for 2 minutes, then stir in remaining butter.
4. **Combine:** Return shrimp to the skillet and toss with sauce. Add cooked pasta and parsley. Toss to combine.
5. **Serve:** Serve immediately.

Chicken Pot Pie

Ingredients:

- 2 cups cooked chicken, diced
- 1 cup frozen peas and carrots
- 1/2 cup onion, chopped
- 1/2 cup celery, chopped
- 1/4 cup butter
- 1/4 cup all-purpose flour
- 1 cup chicken broth
- 1 cup milk
- 1 tsp dried thyme
- 1 pre-made pie crust
- Salt and pepper to taste

Instructions:

1. **Preheat Oven:** Preheat oven to 425°F (220°C).
2. **Prepare Filling:** In a large saucepan, melt butter over medium heat. Add onion and celery and cook until softened. Stir in flour and cook for 1 minute. Gradually add chicken broth and milk, stirring constantly. Cook until thickened. Stir in chicken, peas, carrots, and thyme. Season with salt and pepper.
3. **Assemble Pie:** Pour filling into a pie dish. Place pie crust over the filling and trim excess. Cut slits in the crust for steam to escape.
4. **Bake:** Bake for 30-35 minutes, or until crust is golden brown and filling is bubbly.
5. **Serve:** Let cool for a few minutes before serving.

Sausage and Peppers Pasta

Ingredients:

- 12 oz pasta (penne or rigatoni)
- 1 lb Italian sausage, sliced
- 1 red bell pepper, sliced
- 1 green bell pepper, sliced
- 1 onion, sliced
- 2 garlic cloves, minced
- 1 cup marinara sauce
- 2 tbsp olive oil
- 1/4 cup grated Parmesan cheese
- Salt and pepper to taste

Instructions:

1. **Cook Pasta:** Cook pasta according to package instructions. Drain and set aside.
2. **Cook Sausage:** In a large skillet, heat olive oil over medium heat. Add sausage and cook until browned. Remove from skillet and set aside.
3. **Cook Vegetables:** In the same skillet, add bell peppers, onion, and garlic. Cook until softened.
4. **Combine Ingredients:** Return sausage to the skillet and stir in marinara sauce. Cook for 5 minutes. Toss in cooked pasta and Parmesan cheese.
5. **Serve:** Serve hot.

Thai Peanut Chicken

Ingredients:

- 1 lb chicken breast, cut into strips
- 1/2 cup creamy peanut butter
- 1/4 cup soy sauce
- 2 tbsp honey
- 2 tbsp rice vinegar
- 1 garlic clove, minced
- 1 tbsp fresh ginger, minced
- 2 tbsp vegetable oil
- 1/4 cup chopped peanuts
- 1/4 cup chopped cilantro (optional)

Instructions:

1. **Prepare Sauce:** In a bowl, mix together peanut butter, soy sauce, honey, rice vinegar, garlic, and ginger.
2. **Cook Chicken:** Heat vegetable oil in a large skillet over medium heat. Add chicken and cook until no longer pink, about 5-7 minutes.
3. **Add Sauce:** Stir in peanut sauce and cook for another 3-4 minutes, until chicken is well coated and heated through.
4. **Serve:** Garnish with chopped peanuts and cilantro if desired. Serve over rice or noodles.

Pork Chops with Apples and Onions

Ingredients:

- 4 bone-in pork chops
- 2 apples, sliced
- 1 onion, sliced
- 2 tbsp olive oil
- 1/2 cup chicken broth
- 1 tbsp fresh thyme leaves
- 2 tbsp brown sugar
- Salt and pepper to taste

Instructions:

1. **Preheat Oven:** Preheat oven to 375°F (190°C).
2. **Sear Pork Chops:** Heat olive oil in a large ovenproof skillet over medium-high heat. Season pork chops with salt and pepper and sear for 4-5 minutes per side, until golden brown. Remove and set aside.
3. **Cook Apples and Onions:** In the same skillet, add onions and apples. Cook until softened. Stir in brown sugar and thyme.
4. **Add Broth and Return Pork Chops:** Pour in chicken broth and return pork chops to the skillet.
5. **Bake:** Transfer skillet to the oven and bake for 20-25 minutes, or until pork chops reach an internal temperature of 145°F (63°C).
6. **Serve:** Serve pork chops with apples and onions spooned over the top.

One-Pot Pasta Primavera

Ingredients:

- 12 oz pasta (penne, fusilli, or your choice)
- 2 cups mixed vegetables (bell peppers, zucchini, cherry tomatoes)
- 3 garlic cloves, minced
- 1/4 cup olive oil
- 1 cup vegetable broth
- 1 cup heavy cream
- 1/2 cup grated Parmesan cheese
- Salt and pepper to taste
- Fresh basil for garnish (optional)

Instructions:

1. **Cook Vegetables:** Heat olive oil in a large pot over medium heat. Add garlic and cook until fragrant. Add mixed vegetables and cook until tender.
2. **Add Pasta and Broth:** Add pasta and vegetable broth to the pot. Bring to a boil, then reduce heat and simmer until pasta is cooked and most of the broth is absorbed.
3. **Prepare Sauce:** Stir in heavy cream and Parmesan cheese. Cook until the sauce is creamy and pasta is well coated.
4. **Serve:** Season with salt and pepper. Garnish with fresh basil if desired.

Chicken and Black Bean Enchiladas

Ingredients:

- 2 cups cooked, shredded chicken
- 1 can (15 oz) black beans, drained and rinsed
- 1 cup shredded cheddar cheese
- 1 cup enchilada sauce
- 8 flour tortillas
- 1/2 cup chopped cilantro
- 1/2 cup sour cream (optional)

Instructions:

1. **Preheat Oven:** Preheat oven to 375°F (190°C).
2. **Prepare Filling:** In a bowl, mix together chicken, black beans, and 1/2 cup of cheese.
3. **Assemble Enchiladas:** Spoon filling onto tortillas, roll them up, and place them seam-side down in a greased baking dish.
4. **Add Sauce and Cheese:** Pour enchilada sauce over the top and sprinkle with remaining cheese.
5. **Bake:** Bake for 20-25 minutes, or until cheese is melted and bubbly.
6. **Serve:** Garnish with chopped cilantro and a dollop of sour cream if desired.

Buffalo Chicken Salad

Ingredients:

- 2 cups cooked, shredded chicken
- 1/4 cup buffalo sauce
- 4 cups mixed salad greens
- 1 cup cherry tomatoes, halved
- 1/2 cup celery, chopped
- 1/4 cup crumbled blue cheese
- 1/4 cup ranch or blue cheese dressing

Instructions:

1. **Prepare Chicken:** Toss shredded chicken with buffalo sauce.
2. **Assemble Salad:** In a large bowl, combine salad greens, cherry tomatoes, and celery. Top with buffalo chicken and crumbled blue cheese.
3. **Serve:** Drizzle with ranch or blue cheese dressing and serve immediately.

Creamy Garlic Parmesan Orzo

Ingredients:

- 1 cup orzo pasta
- 2 tbsp butter
- 3 garlic cloves, minced
- 1/2 cup heavy cream
- 1/2 cup grated Parmesan cheese
- 1/4 cup chopped parsley (optional)
- Salt and pepper to taste

Instructions:

1. **Cook Orzo:** Cook orzo according to package instructions. Drain and set aside.
2. **Prepare Sauce:** In a large skillet, melt butter over medium heat. Add garlic and cook until fragrant. Stir in heavy cream and cook for 2 minutes.
3. **Add Orzo and Cheese:** Stir in cooked orzo and Parmesan cheese. Cook until well combined and heated through.
4. **Serve:** Season with salt and pepper and garnish with chopped parsley if desired.

Fish Tacos with Lime Crema

Ingredients:

- 1 lb white fish fillets (such as cod or tilapia)
- 1/4 cup olive oil
- 1 tsp chili powder
- 1 tsp cumin
- 1/2 tsp paprika
- 1/2 tsp garlic powder
- 8 small tortillas
- 1 cup shredded cabbage
- 1/4 cup chopped cilantro
- 1/2 cup sour cream
- 2 tbsp lime juice

Instructions:

1. **Prepare Fish:** Preheat grill or oven to 400°F (200°C). Brush fish fillets with olive oil and season with chili powder, cumin, paprika, and garlic powder.
2. **Cook Fish:** Grill or bake fish for 10-12 minutes, or until cooked through. Flake into pieces.
3. **Prepare Lime Crema:** In a bowl, mix sour cream with lime juice.
4. **Assemble Tacos:** Place shredded cabbage on tortillas, top with fish, and drizzle with lime crema. Garnish with chopped cilantro.
5. **Serve:** Serve immediately.

Stuffed Zucchini Boats

Ingredients:

- 4 medium zucchinis
- 1/2 lb ground beef or turkey
- 1/2 cup onion, chopped
- 1 cup marinara sauce
- 1/2 cup shredded mozzarella cheese
- 1/4 cup grated Parmesan cheese
- 2 tbsp olive oil
- Salt and pepper to taste

Instructions:

1. **Preheat Oven:** Preheat oven to 375°F (190°C).
2. **Prepare Zucchini:** Cut zucchinis in half lengthwise and scoop out the center to create boats. Brush with olive oil and season with salt and pepper.
3. **Cook Filling:** In a skillet, cook ground beef or turkey with onion until browned. Drain excess fat and stir in marinara sauce.
4. **Stuff Zucchini:** Fill zucchini boats with meat mixture and top with mozzarella and Parmesan cheese.
5. **Bake:** Bake for 20-25 minutes, or until zucchini is tender and cheese is melted.
6. **Serve:** Serve hot.

Chicken Cacciatore

Ingredients:

- 4 chicken thighs
- 1 cup sliced mushrooms
- 1 bell pepper, chopped
- 1 onion, chopped
- 2 garlic cloves, minced
- 1 can (14.5 oz) diced tomatoes
- 1/2 cup white wine (optional)
- 1 tsp dried oregano
- 1 tsp dried basil
- 2 tbsp olive oil
- Salt and pepper to taste

Instructions:

1. **Cook Chicken:** Heat olive oil in a large skillet over medium heat. Add chicken thighs and cook until browned on both sides. Remove and set aside.
2. **Prepare Sauce:** In the same skillet, cook onion, bell pepper, mushrooms, and garlic until softened. Stir in diced tomatoes, white wine (if using), oregano, and basil.
3. **Simmer:** Return chicken to the skillet and simmer for 20-25 minutes, or until chicken is cooked through and sauce has thickened.
4. **Serve:** Serve with pasta, rice, or crusty bread.

Sweet Chili Meatballs

Ingredients:

- 1 lb ground beef
- 1/2 cup breadcrumbs
- 1/4 cup grated Parmesan cheese
- 1/4 cup chopped fresh parsley
- 1 egg
- 1/2 cup sweet chili sauce
- 2 tbsp soy sauce
- 2 garlic cloves, minced
- Salt and pepper to taste

Instructions:

1. **Preheat Oven:** Preheat oven to 400°F (200°C).
2. **Mix Meatballs:** In a bowl, combine ground beef, breadcrumbs, Parmesan cheese, parsley, egg, salt, and pepper. Mix until well combined.
3. **Form Meatballs:** Shape mixture into 1-inch meatballs and place on a baking sheet.
4. **Bake:** Bake for 15-20 minutes, or until meatballs are cooked through.
5. **Prepare Sauce:** In a small bowl, mix sweet chili sauce, soy sauce, and garlic.
6. **Toss Meatballs:** Toss cooked meatballs in the sauce. Serve hot.

Broccoli and Cheddar Stuffed Chicken

Ingredients:

- 4 boneless, skinless chicken breasts
- 1 cup broccoli florets, steamed and chopped
- 1/2 cup shredded cheddar cheese
- 1/4 cup cream cheese, softened
- 1/2 tsp garlic powder
- 1/2 tsp onion powder
- Salt and pepper to taste
- 1 tbsp olive oil

Instructions:

1. **Preheat Oven:** Preheat oven to 375°F (190°C).
2. **Prepare Filling:** In a bowl, mix together chopped broccoli, cheddar cheese, cream cheese, garlic powder, and onion powder.
3. **Stuff Chicken:** Cut a pocket into each chicken breast and stuff with the broccoli mixture. Season with salt and pepper.
4. **Sear Chicken:** Heat olive oil in a skillet over medium-high heat. Sear chicken breasts for 2-3 minutes per side until golden brown.
5. **Bake:** Transfer chicken to a baking dish and bake for 20-25 minutes, or until chicken reaches an internal temperature of 165°F (74°C).
6. **Serve:** Serve hot.

Spicy Sausage Pasta

Ingredients:

- 12 oz pasta (penne or rigatoni)
- 1 lb spicy Italian sausage, sliced
- 1 cup marinara sauce
- 1/2 cup heavy cream
- 1/2 cup grated Parmesan cheese
- 1/2 tsp red pepper flakes (optional)
- 2 tbsp olive oil
- Salt and pepper to taste

Instructions:

1. **Cook Pasta:** Cook pasta according to package instructions. Drain and set aside.
2. **Cook Sausage:** In a large skillet, heat olive oil over medium heat. Add sausage and cook until browned.
3. **Prepare Sauce:** Stir in marinara sauce and red pepper flakes if using. Cook for 2-3 minutes.
4. **Combine Ingredients:** Add heavy cream and Parmesan cheese, stirring until the sauce is creamy. Toss in cooked pasta and mix well.
5. **Serve:** Serve hot.

Cheesy Chicken and Rice Bake

Ingredients:

- 2 cups cooked chicken, diced
- 1 cup cooked rice
- 1 cup shredded cheddar cheese
- 1 cup cream of chicken soup
- 1/2 cup milk
- 1/2 cup frozen peas
- 1/2 cup chopped onion
- 1/2 tsp garlic powder
- Salt and pepper to taste
- 1/2 cup breadcrumbs

Instructions:

1. **Preheat Oven:** Preheat oven to 375°F (190°C).
2. **Mix Ingredients:** In a bowl, combine chicken, rice, cheddar cheese, cream of chicken soup, milk, peas, onion, garlic powder, salt, and pepper.
3. **Transfer to Dish:** Pour mixture into a greased baking dish.
4. **Top and Bake:** Sprinkle breadcrumbs over the top. Bake for 25-30 minutes, or until bubbly and the top is golden brown.
5. **Serve:** Serve hot.

Shrimp and Grits

Ingredients:

- 1 lb shrimp, peeled and deveined
- 1 cup grits
- 2 cups chicken broth
- 1 cup milk
- 4 tbsp butter
- 1/2 cup shredded cheddar cheese
- 2 garlic cloves, minced
- 1/2 tsp paprika
- 1/4 tsp cayenne pepper (optional)
- 2 tbsp olive oil
- Salt and pepper to taste
- Chopped green onions for garnish

Instructions:

1. **Cook Grits:** In a saucepan, bring chicken broth and milk to a boil. Stir in grits and reduce heat. Cook according to package instructions, stirring occasionally. Stir in butter and cheddar cheese.
2. **Cook Shrimp:** In a skillet, heat olive oil over medium heat. Add garlic and cook until fragrant. Add shrimp, paprika, cayenne pepper if using, salt, and pepper. Cook for 2-3 minutes per side, until shrimp are pink and cooked through.
3. **Serve:** Serve shrimp over a bed of creamy grits. Garnish with chopped green onions.

BBQ Meatloaf

Ingredients:

- 1 lb ground beef
- 1/2 cup breadcrumbs
- 1/2 cup barbecue sauce
- 1/2 cup chopped onion
- 1 egg
- 2 garlic cloves, minced
- 1/2 tsp dried thyme
- Salt and pepper to taste

Instructions:

1. **Preheat Oven:** Preheat oven to 375°F (190°C).
2. **Prepare Meatloaf:** In a large bowl, combine ground beef, breadcrumbs, barbecue sauce, onion, egg, garlic, thyme, salt, and pepper. Mix until well combined.
3. **Shape and Bake:** Form mixture into a loaf and place in a greased baking dish. Bake for 45-50 minutes, or until the internal temperature reaches 160°F (71°C).
4. **Serve:** Let meatloaf rest for a few minutes before slicing and serving.

Sweet Chili Meatballs

Ingredients:

- 1 lb ground beef
- 1/2 cup breadcrumbs
- 1/4 cup grated Parmesan cheese
- 1/4 cup chopped fresh parsley
- 1 egg
- 1/2 cup sweet chili sauce
- 2 tbsp soy sauce
- 2 garlic cloves, minced
- Salt and pepper to taste

Instructions:

1. **Preheat Oven:** Preheat oven to 400°F (200°C).
2. **Mix Meatballs:** In a bowl, combine ground beef, breadcrumbs, Parmesan cheese, parsley, egg, salt, and pepper. Mix until well combined.
3. **Form Meatballs:** Shape mixture into 1-inch meatballs and place on a baking sheet.
4. **Bake:** Bake for 15-20 minutes, or until meatballs are cooked through.
5. **Prepare Sauce:** In a small bowl, mix sweet chili sauce, soy sauce, and garlic.
6. **Toss Meatballs:** Toss cooked meatballs in the sauce. Serve hot.

Broccoli and Cheddar Stuffed Chicken

Ingredients:

- 4 boneless, skinless chicken breasts
- 1 cup broccoli florets, steamed and chopped
- 1/2 cup shredded cheddar cheese
- 1/4 cup cream cheese, softened
- 1/2 tsp garlic powder
- 1/2 tsp onion powder
- Salt and pepper to taste
- 1 tbsp olive oil

Instructions:

1. **Preheat Oven:** Preheat oven to 375°F (190°C).
2. **Prepare Filling:** In a bowl, mix together chopped broccoli, cheddar cheese, cream cheese, garlic powder, and onion powder.
3. **Stuff Chicken:** Cut a pocket into each chicken breast and stuff with the broccoli mixture. Season with salt and pepper.
4. **Sear Chicken:** Heat olive oil in a skillet over medium-high heat. Sear chicken breasts for 2-3 minutes per side until golden brown.
5. **Bake:** Transfer chicken to a baking dish and bake for 20-25 minutes, or until chicken reaches an internal temperature of 165°F (74°C).
6. **Serve:** Serve hot.

Spicy Sausage Pasta

Ingredients:

- 12 oz pasta (penne or rigatoni)
- 1 lb spicy Italian sausage, sliced
- 1 cup marinara sauce
- 1/2 cup heavy cream
- 1/2 cup grated Parmesan cheese
- 1/2 tsp red pepper flakes (optional)
- 2 tbsp olive oil
- Salt and pepper to taste

Instructions:

1. **Cook Pasta:** Cook pasta according to package instructions. Drain and set aside.
2. **Cook Sausage:** In a large skillet, heat olive oil over medium heat. Add sausage and cook until browned.
3. **Prepare Sauce:** Stir in marinara sauce and red pepper flakes if using. Cook for 2-3 minutes.
4. **Combine Ingredients:** Add heavy cream and Parmesan cheese, stirring until the sauce is creamy. Toss in cooked pasta and mix well.
5. **Serve:** Serve hot.

Cheesy Chicken and Rice Bake

Ingredients:

- 2 cups cooked chicken, diced
- 1 cup cooked rice
- 1 cup shredded cheddar cheese
- 1 cup cream of chicken soup
- 1/2 cup milk
- 1/2 cup frozen peas
- 1/2 cup chopped onion
- 1/2 tsp garlic powder
- Salt and pepper to taste
- 1/2 cup breadcrumbs

Instructions:

1. **Preheat Oven:** Preheat oven to 375°F (190°C).
2. **Mix Ingredients:** In a bowl, combine chicken, rice, cheddar cheese, cream of chicken soup, milk, peas, onion, garlic powder, salt, and pepper.
3. **Transfer to Dish:** Pour mixture into a greased baking dish.
4. **Top and Bake:** Sprinkle breadcrumbs over the top. Bake for 25-30 minutes, or until bubbly and the top is golden brown.
5. **Serve:** Serve hot.

Shrimp and Grits

Ingredients:

- 1 lb shrimp, peeled and deveined
- 1 cup grits
- 2 cups chicken broth
- 1 cup milk
- 4 tbsp butter
- 1/2 cup shredded cheddar cheese
- 2 garlic cloves, minced
- 1/2 tsp paprika
- 1/4 tsp cayenne pepper (optional)
- 2 tbsp olive oil
- Salt and pepper to taste
- Chopped green onions for garnish

Instructions:

1. **Cook Grits:** In a saucepan, bring chicken broth and milk to a boil. Stir in grits and reduce heat. Cook according to package instructions, stirring occasionally. Stir in butter and cheddar cheese.
2. **Cook Shrimp:** In a skillet, heat olive oil over medium heat. Add garlic and cook until fragrant. Add shrimp, paprika, cayenne pepper if using, salt, and pepper. Cook for 2-3 minutes per side, until shrimp are pink and cooked through.
3. **Serve:** Serve shrimp over a bed of creamy grits. Garnish with chopped green onions.

BBQ Meatloaf

Ingredients:

- 1 lb ground beef
- 1/2 cup breadcrumbs
- 1/2 cup barbecue sauce
- 1/2 cup chopped onion
- 1 egg
- 2 garlic cloves, minced
- 1/2 tsp dried thyme
- Salt and pepper to taste

Instructions:

1. **Preheat Oven:** Preheat oven to 375°F (190°C).
2. **Prepare Meatloaf:** In a large bowl, combine ground beef, breadcrumbs, barbecue sauce, onion, egg, garlic, thyme, salt, and pepper. Mix until well combined.
3. **Shape and Bake:** Form mixture into a loaf and place in a greased baking dish. Bake for 45-50 minutes, or until the internal temperature reaches 160°F (71°C).
4. **Serve:** Let meatloaf rest for a few minutes before slicing and serving.